Mary Dana Shindler

**The Western harp**

A collection of Sunday music, consisting of sacred words adapted to classic

and popular airs

Mary Dana Shindler

**The Western harp**
*A collection of Sunday music, consisting of sacred words adapted to classic and popular airs*

ISBN/EAN: 9783337102050

Printed in Europe, USA, Canada, Australia, Japan

Cover: Foto ©Thomas Meinert / pixelio.de

More available books at **www.hansebooks.com**

# THE

# WESTERN HARP:

A COLLECTION OF

# SUNDAY MUSIC:

CONSISTING OF

## SACRED WORDS ADAPTED TO

# CLASSIC AND POPULAR AIRS,

AND ARRANGED FOR THE

# PIANO-FORTE.

WORDS BY

## MRS. M. S. B. DANA SHINDLER.

AUTHOR OF THE NORTHERN AND SOUTHERN HARPS, &c.

## BOSTON:
### PUBLISHED BY OLIVER DITSON & COMPANY,
277 WASHINGTON STREET.

# PREFACE.

The author has always found it difficult to obtain a sufficient supply of Sunday music, arranged for the Piano. This book, together with the Northern and Southern Harps, now provides sacred songs, duetts, and trios, in great abundance and variety. Books of sacred music every where exist, but they generally require considerable knowledge of harmony, and a number of voices; and when THE SOUTHERN HARP—the first of the series—appeared, several years ago, it was considered a desideratum, and was eminently successful. Many players like to devote a portion of their Sunday time to private sacred song, and wish to call in the aid of their instruments in the delightful employment; to such I dedicate these works, and trust that they will receive both pleasure and profit from their constant use,

M. S. B. DANA SHINDLER.

# CONTENTS.

# THE GREAT SALVATION.

DUET.

S. Glover.

1. Sing me the great sal - va - tion, Bought by the Sa - vior's blood ; And
2. Ne'er slumber-ing nor sleep-ing, God keepeth watch and ward ; He

tell how from eve - ry na - tion, Shall sound forth the praise of God?
will, eve - ry prom - ise keep-ing, See earth to his love re - stored.

Men groping now in blind - ness, Soon shall his glo - ry see, And be
Then in a world of dan - - gers, We will not yield to fear, We are

saved by his lov - ing kind - ness, And made thro' his mer - cy, free .... And be
pil - grims and we are stran - gers, But Je - sus is ev - er near....... We are

saved by his lov - ing kind - ness, And made thro' his mercy free ....
pil - grims and we are stran - - gers, But Je - sus is ev - er near.........

Dim.

1st VOICE.
PIU ANIMATO.

Ev - er God's prai - ses sounding; Loud let our voi - ces ring, ...
Ev - er with hu - man feel - ing; Je - sus will sym - pa - thize,......

ev - er his love a - bounding,
ev - er the tears, down steal - ing,

Let us to - geth - er sing! . . .
We'll wipe from all our eyes,......

**AGITATO.**

Mer-cy the Lord be - tow - eth,
One with the Son and Fath - - er,

Free-ly a - like too all,
One with the spir - it to,

And the
We may

fountain of life out-flow - eth,
cheer - ful - ly com - fort gath - er,

Both for great, and small ;
For God's word is true.

And the
We may

foun - tain of    life    out - flow - eth,   Both   for    great,   for great and   small.
cheer - ful - ly   com - fort   gath - er,   For   God's word, God's word is    true.

LENTO.                Rall. a tempo.

Yes!        yes, yes!      Yes! yes, 'tis a great   sal - - va - tion,    The

Yes!        yes, yes!      Yes! yes, 'tis a great   sal - - va - tion,    The

LENTO.                Rall. a tempo.

purchase of Je - sus' blood,     And soon may each tongue and na - tion, Sound forth the praise of

purchase of Je - sus' blood,     And soon may each tongue and na - tion, Sound forth the praise of

God!     And soon may each tongue and na - - tion, Sound forth the praise of God!

God!     And soon may each tongue and na - - tion, Sound forth the praise of God!

# SAINTS AND ANGELS.

Donizetti.

Saints and an - gels join in one, With sweetest har - mo - ny...... To

praise the great Re - deemer's name; Who died for you and me. Let us of - fer with

glad hearts, Our hum - ble songs to Heav - en; And thank the Lord u - nit - ed - ly,.... For all his mer - cies giv'n. Saints and an - gels join in one, To praise the great Redeemer's name, Who died for you and

me. Saints and angels join in one, To praise the great Redeemer's . . . . . name, Who died for you and me, you and me.

## 2.

All on earth and all in heaven,
Who love the Savior's name,
Unite with joy to sing his praise,
And all his praise proclaim.
Though our sad hearts may now mourn,
We'll raise our song to heaven;
For God has promised faithfully,
Our sins shall be forgiv'n.
'Saints and angels join in one,
To praise the great Redeemer's name,
Who died for you and me.

# HARK! THE PASSING BELL.

Stephen Glover.

Hark! the pas-sing bell, Mourn-ful-ly and slow, Sounds its sol-emn knell; Speaks of earth-ly woe! Let it not in vain, Give its warn-ing sound; When 'tis heard a-gain,...... Where may you be found? For the days of man, ....   E - - - vil are and few;   Oh! how quickly then,   Its

knell may be for you?   Oh! how quickly then, ....   Its knell may be for   you.

### 2.

For that solemn hour,
Always ready be;
Armed with sudden power,
Death may come to thee!
Trust thy Father's love,
Live a life of prayer,
Ever look above,
For thy home is there.
But wouldst thou be sure
Of that bright abode,
Then delay no more,
Prepare to meet thy God!

## LET ME GO FAR AWAY.

I. B. Woodbury.

1. Let me go far a - way from the anguish of earth, From the dark weary land which to sorrow gives birth; Let me bid glad fare - well to this weeping and

woe,    Far a - way from this world    let me go,  let    me    go!  Far a -

Ritard.

way from this world    let me    go,    let me    go!

2 But I want not away from my sorrows to flee,
   Till my heart has been won, O my Savior! to Thee!
   When I love Thee, my God! love my friend and my foe,
   Then, O then, can I pray, let me go, let me go!

3 When the battle of life has been fought and been won,
   When the Savior can say to me, "Thou hast well done!"
   When the Master has nought to detain me below,
   Then, O then will I pray, let me go, let me go!

4 I am longing to sing with the angels above,
   With the saints and the martyrs, Christ's wonderful love;
   I am longing with them at His feet to bow low,
   My impatience forgive; let me go, let me go!

# WHENE'ER I'M PRAYING.

Abt.

ALLEGRO. MODERATO.

1. There's many a voice di - vine, Speaks to this soul of mine, There's many a

*mf*

voice di - vine, Speaks to this soul of mine, De - light-ful words of comfort say - ing, They fill me

with de-light, At morning, noon, or night; Those words they're say - ing Whene'er I'm praying, They fill me

*p* Legato.

Cres.

**2.**

‖: The trusting heart can pray
Either by night or day ; :‖
Though not a word the lips are saying ;
‖: Faith's eye, in every place,
Can see the Father's face,
Sweet words he's saying
Whene'er I'm praying. :‖

**3.**

‖: If Him I could not see,
Earth would be dark to me, :‖
Sad words would every thing be saying ;
‖: But when I trust in Him,
Shines forth a glorious beam ;
Kind words He's saying,
Whene'er I'm praying. :‖

# HOLY FATHER.

## DUET.

A. Garaude.

Ho - ly Fa -- ther hear.... us sigh - - - ing, For thy pard - 'ning mer - - cy

Ho - ly Fa -- ther hear.... us sigh - - - ing, For thy pard - 'ning mer - - cy

cry - - ing, Full of sor - row, here we lan - guish, Leave us not in hope - less

cry - - ing, Full of sor - row, here we lan - guish, Leave us not in hope - less an - - guish! Full of sor - row here we lan - guish, Leave us not in hope - less

an - - guish! Full of sor - row here we lan - guish, Leave us not in hope - less

an - guish!

an - guish!

**2.**
Holy Father! we come boldly,
Oh, do not repulse us coldly!
:||: Stretch thy kind arms to recieve us,
And of all these woes releive us! :||

**3.**
Holy Father! when we're straying,
Thy good laws no more obeying,
:||: Then in mercy wilt thou call us;
Lest more bitter griefs befall us! :||

**4.**
Holy Father! we are strangers
In a world all full of dangers;
:||: May thy watchful care be o'er us,
Till we reach the house before us! :||

# CHARITY.

Brinley Richards.

1. Will you come and join with me, In the praise of Chari - ty? Will you
2. Oh, may I be filled with thee, Humble, ho - ly Chari - ty! Oh, may

1. Will you come and join with me, In the praise of Chari - ty? Will you
2. Oh, may I be filled with thee, Humble, ho - ly Chari - ty! Oh, may

come and join with me, In the praise of Chari - ty? Which loveth
I be filled with thee, Humble, ho - ly Chari - ty! Be kind to

come and join with me, In the praise of Chari - ty? Which loveth still, Which loveth
I be filled with thee, Humble, ho - ly Chari - ty! Be kind to all, Be kind to

still,                Thro' good and ill?  Where the  Christian virtues  be,.... 'Tis the
all,                 Both great and small.  May  it  my  endeav-or  be,.... Far from

still,  Thro' good and ill,  Thro' good and ill?  Where the  Christian virtues  be,.... 'Tis the
all,  Both great and small,  Both great and small.  May  it  my  endeav-or  be,.... Far from

great-est of the     Where   the   Chris - tian virtues  be,.... 'Tis the  fair - est of the
sin - ful pride to   May   it   my   endeav-or   be,...... Far from sin - ful pride to

great-est of the three.  Where  the  Chris - tian virtues  be,.... 'Tis the  fair - est of the
sin - ful pride to flee,  May   it   my   endeav-or   be,...... Far from sin - ful pride to

three; And it feareth to of - fend, And it lov - eth foe and friend;
flee; And may Faith, and Hope, and Love, Never from my heart re . move;

three;
flee;

And it
But be

And it suffers long, Under
But be treasured there, With an

suffers long, Under harm and wrong, And a - bi - deth to the end; And it suffers long, Under
treasured there With an honest care, Till I reach my home a - bove; But be treasured there With an

harm and wrong, And a - bi - deth to the end; And it  suffers long, Under harm and wrong, And a-
honest care, Till I    reach   my home a - bove; But  be treasured there With an   honest care, Till I

harm and wrong, And a - bi - deth to the end; And it  suffers long, Under harm and wrong, And a-
honest care, Till I    reach   my home a - bove; But  be treasured there With an   honest care, Till I

bi - deth to the end, And    a - bi -  deth to the end, And     a - bi - deth to the end.
reach my home a - bove, Till    I  reach   my home a - bove, Till    I  reach  my home a - bove.

bi - deth to the end, And    a - bi -  deth to the end, And     a - bi - deth to the end.
reach my home a - bove, Till    I  reach   my home a - bove, Till    I  reach  my home a - bove.

# LIKE HOLY ANGELS.

Music by F. Romer.

Like ho - ly an - gels of the Lord, Oh, let us learn to do his will, With earn-est

hearts to keep his word, And glad-ly his commands ful - fil, And glad - ly his commands ful -

- fil. A - like in an - guish and in joy, He's to his chil - dren ev - er near; No sor - row shall their faith des - troy, And they will nev - er yield to fear. Like ho - ly an - - - gels of the

Lord, Oh, let us learn to do his will, Oh, let us learn to do.......... ............ his will.

### 2.

I'll bravely gird my armor on,
  With courage fight each deadly foe
Soon life's hard battle will be won,
:||: And I shall bid farewell to woe. :||
If calmly trusting in the Lord,
  We pass away life's fleeting years,
We'll not forget his blessed word,
  We'll soothe our sorrows, dry our tears.
  Like holy angels, &c.

# THE CHRISTIAN'S REFUGE.

Franz Abt.

1. All a-round us dan-gers rise, While a-bove us, from the
2. Drooping thus, and lan-guish-ing, E'en the warm and cheer-ful

skies; Life's frail bark is tem-pest-tost, All is o-ver, all is
spring Brought no sun - shine to my breast, Na - ture all in gloom was

lost. Thus com-plain - ing, and for-lorn, Mourn'd I from the ear-ly
drest. I was blind, and cold, and dead, E - ven hope from me had

morn, . . . . . . . . Mourn'd   I . . . . through   the   live - - long
fied; . . . . . . . . . But   the   Sa - . - vior   called   to

night,   Could   not   see . . . . . . . . .   the heav'n - ly
me,   Said,   "I   will . . . . . . . .   thy re - fuge

light;"   Could   not   see . . . . . .   the heav'n - ly   light.
be;"   Said,   "I   will . . . . . .   thy re - fuge be."

**3.**

"In my Church thou may'st abide,
There behold me crucified,
There behold me ris'n again,
Bringing life to wretched men,

Life of body, life of soul,
Making all the wounded whole!"
To the Savior then I flew;
I have found His promise true!

# MORNING SONG.

Verdi.

When the first morning light Comes with its beam so bright, Chasing the gloom of night,

Lord, we a - dore thee! Hear us while thus we pray, Turn us from sin a - way; Keep us through-

out this day, Lord, we im - plore thee! Fa - ther be - friend us, Al - ways de - fend us!

2.

In Thee may we abide,
For every want provide,
Be thou our guard and guide,
While on earth roaming!
May we all means employ,
Sin in us to destroy;
Then shall we hail with joy,
Thy second coming!
    Father defend us, &c.

# CHRIST IS RISEN.

Henry Russell.

1. Sons of God! raise high your hearts and voi - ces ! Jesus has burst the bondage of the grave!
2. Sons of God! the Sa - vior has as .- cend - ed! Gaze up to heaven and see his glory there!

Hail to the day, all earth and heav'n re-joic - es ! Je-sus arose, who died the world to save ! Why
There doth he reign, by an - gel hosts at - tend - ed! Praise be to God! we may that glo - ry share! So,

should the spir-it on the earth be droop - ing? Why should her wings be dragging in the mire?
mid earth's trouble we'll our Lord re - mem - ber, What was our gain, wo'll count it all but loss;

Why, should the soul  to earthly things be stooping, When 'tis her glo-ry heav'nward to  as-pire ?
Oh ;  what de-light  to join that bless-ed num - ber, Who count it  joy with  him to bear the cross !

Sing  we  then  our Savior's re - sur-rection ! Sing we  then  with voi-ces loud and free !
Sing  we  then  our Savior's re - sur-rection ! Sing we  then  with voi-ces loud and free !

Sing   we   then,    a-way with all  de - jec-tion ! Sing we then of our  im - mor-tal - i - ty.
Sing   we   then,    a - way with all de - jec-tion ! Sing we then of  our  im - mor - tal - i - ty.

# THE SPIRIT HOME.

M. Bartholdy.

**Allegretto con Moto.**

1. Oh, why should my glorious soul Be con - - fined to this gloomy
2. Oh, why should I lon - ger live With my spir - it enchained be-

3. Oh, why in the world's broad road Should I proud - ly and mad-ly
4. I'll fly to my spir - it home, 'Tis a pleas - ant and safe a-

earth, When up - ward it might be soar - ing, The child of a heaven-ly
low, When voi - ces from heaven are call - ing A way from this world of

stay, When God by his love is point - ing, My feet to the nar - row
bode; I'll fly to my saints' com - mun - ion, I'll fly to the church of

Cres.

Cres.

birth?    When    up - ward it might be soar - ing,    The    child    of a heavenly
woe ?    When    voi - ces from heaven are call - ing    A - way    from this world of

way ?    When    God    by his love is point - ing    My    feet    to the nar-row
God,    I'll    fly    to the saints' com-mun - ion,    I'll    fly    to the church of

birth?    a heavenly birth ?      The child    of a heavenly birth.
woe ?    this world of woe,      A - way    from this world of woe.

way ?    the nar - row way,    My feet    to the nar - row way.
God,    the church of God,    I'll fly    to the church of God.

# OH! TURN US NOT AWAY.

TRIO.

Music by Bellini.

ANDANTE CON ESPRESSIONE.

1. Je - sus, thou Sa - vior! bow down thine ear! We kneel be - fore thee, tremb - ling with fear;

2. Thou, who in an - guish fast - ed and prayed, Who wast re - ject - ed, tempt - ed, betrayed,

Hast thou not prom - ised our prayer to hear?·········· Our prayer to hear?

Oh, in thy mer - cy, grant us thine aid!··········· grant us thine aid!

hast thou not shed thy pre - cious blood, For all thy hu - man broth - er - hood?

We come to Thee, our great High Priest, Trust - ing thy love, thou Sa - - vior, Christ!

mf
Sure - ly thou wilt not turn us a - way! turn us a - way! A - - -
Sure - ly thou wilt not turn us a - way! turn us a - way! A - - -
turn us, thou wilt not turn us a - way,
p
pp
poco riten.
- way! Oh! turn us not a - way! A - - - way, oh! turn us not a - way!
- way! Oh! turn us not a - way! A - - - way, oh! turn us not a - way!
dim.

# HOPE ON, AND MURMUR NOT.

Stephen Glover.

Hope on, and murmur not,.... In the palace and the cot, Though the
whispered by the breeze,.... As it comes through waving trees, In the

Hope on, and murmur not,.... In the palace and the cot, Though the
whispered by the breeze,.... As it comes through waving trees, In the

sunshine all be gone,.... Let each human heart hope on. In the dreamy hours of
song of ev'-ry bird,...... Are the cheering accents heard. Hark! the wa-ters seem to

sunshine all be gone,.... Let each human heart hope on. In the dreamy hours of
song of ev'-ry bird,...... Are the cheering accents heard. Hark! the wa-ters seem to

night, Hope can give thee vi - sions bright; When the heart feels all a - lone, She can
say,    In their gent-ly murm'-ring play, With a soft and soothing tone, "Wea - ry

night, Hope can give thee vi - sions bright;          When the heart feels all a -
say,    In their gent-ly murm'-ring play,             With a    soft    and    soothing

smile and say, "Hope on !"    Hope    on, She can smile and say,"Hope on," hope on, bope on, hope
heart, hope ev - er    on!"    Hope    on, "Weary heart, hope ev - er on !"  hope on, bope on, hope

lone,    She can smile and  say, "Hope on," She can smile and say,"Hope on," hope on, hope on, hope
tone,    "Wea-ry heart, hope ev - er  on," "Weary heart, hope ev - er  on," hope on, hope on, hope

on !

It is whispered by the

on !

Cres.    Sf

breeze,    As it comes through wav-ing    trees ;.    In the song of eve-ry    bird,    Are the

cheering ac-cents heard. Hark ! the wa-ters seem to    say, ...... In their gen-tly murm'ring play,    With a soft and soothing    tone,..... "Weary heart, weary heart, hope ever on!"

Rall.

A tempo.                                Return to the Sign

Dim.    A tempo.

Hope  on,      hope  on,      hope  on, hope on, hope  on,    It is

Hope  on,      hope  on,      hope  on, hope on, hope  on,...... It is

Dim.    A Tempo.

on, hope on, hope on, hope on, hope on, hope on, hope

on, hope on, hope on, hope on, hope

on, hope on, hope on.

on, hope on, hope on,

# 'TIS WELL.

Franz Abt.

Rather Slow.

1. Let me not, my heaven-ly
2. Thus may I, through thy rich

Fa - ther, Seek the fu - ture to foretell; With more wis - dom
bless - ing, All life's dark - est clouds dis - pel; Through all scenes, how -

let me rath - er From my past ex - pe - rience gath - er, Come what
e'er dis - tress - ing, Let me, my firm faith ex - press - ing, Calm - ly

**3.**
Not one vain, unmeaning sorrow,
  God's dear children ever feel;
From this thought I'll comfort borrow,
Come what will, to-day, to-morrow,
  This I know, 'tis well, 'tis well.

**4.**
When my time has come for dying,
  When I leave this earthly cell,
Then, O then, on God relying,
Will my joyful heart be crying,
  Home at last! 'tis well, 'tis well.

# THINK OF HIM WHO DIED FOR THEE.

Stephen Glover.

1. When thy heart feels sad and wea-ry, And thy dear - - - est friends are
2. There are dear friends watch-ing o'er thee 'Mong the an - - - - gel host a -

dead; . . . When the world seems dark and dreary, And thy bright - - est joys have
bove, . . . . . . There are bright hopes set be-fore thee, Through the Fa - - - ther's ten - der

fied, . . . . . . . . When the fond dreams that you cher - ished, Nought but dreams can ev - er
love, . . . . . . . . Bright-est joys shalt thou in - her - it, Fair-est dreams fulfilled shall

be,            When all   earth - - ly hopes have per - ished, Think of him . . . who died for
be,            If thou wilt,........ with trust-ing   spir - it,   Think of him........I who died for

*pp*    **Dim.**

thee.      Oh! think of him,        Oh! think of him,      Think of him . . . who died for
thee.      Oh! think of him,        Oh!  think of him,     Think of him........ who died  for

a Tempo..          8va. - - - -
*f*  *p*   PED.

thee . . .      Oh! think of him,    Oh think of him,      of him who died      for   thee.
thee . . .      Oh! think of him,    Oh think of him,      of  him who died     for   thee.

PED.        PED.        -Cresc.        *sf*        *f* PED.

# HARK TO THE SABBATH BELLS.

## TRIO.

John Blockley.

1. When the morn is beam - ing O - ver the hills and dells.

2. When the eve is shad - ing O - ver the hills and dells,

1. When the morn is beam - ing O - ver the hills and dells,

Moderato.

_p_

Sweet to wake from dream - ing, Hear - ing the Sabbath bells! All na - ture robed in

Ho - ly vis - ions aid - - ing, Hark to the Sabbath bells ! When comes the peace - ful

Sweet to wake from dream - ing, Hear - ing the Sabbath bells ! All na - ture robed in

Cres.

cheer - ful - ness, In - vites the heart to praise;.... Our Fa - ther God, thy name we bless, For

twi - light hour, We'll sing a song of praise;.... . Our Fa - ther God, we, thee a - dore, For

cheer - ful - ness, In - vites the heart to praise;....

all our Sab - bath days.... When the morn is beam - ing, O - ver the hills and

all our Sab - bath days.... When the eve is shad - ing, O - ver the hills and

When the morn is beam - ing, O - ver the hills and

p

dells,     Sweet   to wake   from   dream - ing,     Hear - ing the Sab - bath

dells,     Ho - ly vis - ions aid - - ing,     Hark   to the Sab - bath

dells,     Sweet   to wake   from   dream - ing,     Hear - ing the Sab - bath

bells !     Hark !     Hark !     Hark   to the Sab - bath

bells !     Hark !     Hark !     Hark   to the Sab - bath

bells !     Hark !     Hark !     Hark   to the Sab - bath

bells!          Hark!          Hark!          Hark to the Sab-bath

bells!          Hark!          Hark!          Hark to the Sab-bath

bells!          Hark!          Hark!          Hark to the Sab-bath

Cres.

bells!

bells!

bells!

Dim.

# THE PEACE OF GOD.

DUET.

Anne Fricker.

1. There is full - ness of joy, there is hope, there is
2. All a - round us are to - - kens of mer - - cy and

love, When we choose for a home the bright world a - bove. There is ful - ness of
peace, And the joys of the Lord will ev - er in-crease.

2nd voice.

All a - round us are

joy, there is hope, there is love, When we choose for a home the bright world a -

to - kens of mer - cy and peace; And the joys of the Lord will ev - er in

1st VOICE. Solo.

love. There's a peace that this world can-not give to the heart, But the
- crease. In the South, in the North, in the East, in the West, God is

Sa - - vior who loves us this peace doth im-part, And from all earthly
giv - - -ing his chil - dren the bless - ing of rest; They who dwell in his

sor - row it ta - keth the smart. There is ful - ness of joy, there is
love are a bund - ant - ly blest.

All a - round us are to - kens of

hope,  There is love,  When we choose for a  home  the bright world a-bove.

mer - - cy and peace,  And the joys  of the Lord  will ev - er in-crease.

High - er than joy . . is God's ho - ly  peace,  And I'll trea - - sure the
Saints  up-on  earth.... and the saints a - bove,  Are to-geth - - er u -

gift  till my life  here shall cease.  'Twas  the last le - - ga-cy
ni - - ling to sing  Je - sus' love,  Bles - sed com - mun - - ion, when

left . . . by the Lord, To the heart that re - ceives it a blessed re -
heart........ can meet heart, And in praise to the Lamb all with rap - ture take
There is full - ness of joy,. there is hope, there is love, When we
- ward.
part. All a - round us are to - - kens of mer - - cy and peace, And the
choose for a home the bright world a - bove.
joys of the Lord will ev - - er in - crease.

# OH! LET US LOVE EACH OTHER.

Nelson.

1st voice.

1. Oh, let us love each oth - er, We who the Sa - vior love, Dwell here with each dear
2. May we all en - vy smoth - er, All strife and an - ger shun, For - giv - ing one an-

2nd voice.

broth - er, As we shall dwell a - bove. Oh yes, for heav-en's bless - ing, Will sure - ly come to
- oth - er, As Christ to us has done. Oh yes, in God con - fid - ing, We need not feel a-

1st voice.

those, Whose char - i - ty, un - ceas - ing, Each day more per-fect grows, We all one Fa - ther
- fraid; While in His love a - bid - ing, Our love is per-fect made, We all one Fa - ther

Cres. Dim.

have,    One fam - i - ly    are we. . . .

Whom Je - ' sus died to    save,    From

Then let    us dwell to - geth  -   er,    As an - gels dwell a -

sin to    set us    free. Then let    us dwell    to - geth  -   er,    As an - gels dwell a -

- bove;  In ; cold and stormy wea - ther, We'll warm our - selves with love, . . .

- bove;  In  cold and stormy wea - ther, We'll warm our - selves with love, . . . The

Is ten - der and is  kind, . . .  Ne'er does  its  neigh - bor

love that suf - fers  long,  Is ten - der and is  kind, . . .

wrong,   But seeks the good to   find,        Then  let  us dwell to - geth  -  er,  As

But seeks the good to   find,        Then  let  us dwell to - geth  -  er,  As

an - gels dwell a - bove;        In   cold and stormy  weath - er, We'll warm our hearts with love.

an - gels dwell a - bove;        In   cold and stormy  weath - er, We'll warm our hearts with love.

*mf  p*                Cres.

# LET US PRAISE THE LORD.

J. P. Ordway.

1. In the work of the Lord a -
2. For he gives us his ho - ly

bound - ing, Our off - 'rings to God let us bring;
Spir - - it, That we may approach him a - right;

And with loud cheerful notes re -
And he gives us a home to in-

sound - - ing, The praise of Je - sus our King. Let us pub - lish the won - drous
her - - - it, When we are pure in his sight. Then to - geth - er his prais - es

sto - - ry, Of the love that was strong-er than death; To his name give the praise and
sing - - - ing, Let our hearts and our voic - es all rise; Till our souls shall with joy be

glo - - - - ry, With all who en - joy life and breath.
spring - - - ing, To en - - joy their bright home in the skies.

CHORUS.
Soprano.
Alto.
1. Let us pub - lish the won - drous sto - - - ry, Of the love that was strong - er than
Tenor.
2. Then to - geth - er our prais - es sing - - - ing, Let our hearts and our voic - es all
Bass.
3. Let us pub - lish the won - drous sto - - - ry, Of the love that was strong - er than
Cres.
death ; To his name give the praise and glo - - ry, With all who en - joy life and breath.
rise, Till our souls shall with joy be spring - ing, To en - joy their bright home in the skies.
death ; To his name give the praise and glo - - ry, With all who en - joy life and breath.
8va.
Ped.
Ped.
Ped.

# AT HOME.

Verdi.

1. Where sin and sor - row never can harm me, Where dwell the hap - py ones, there is my
2. Patient - ly wait - ing, pilgrims and stran - gers, Nothing can frighten us, Nothing can

home; Oh, visions of beau - ty ravish and charm me, Whene'er I think up - on
harm; With spirits all cheer - ful meet we life's dan - gers, E'en to the dark - est days

joys yet to come! There dwell the loved ones long gone be - fore us,
hope lends a charm. Cling we then all to the hope set be - fore us,

Dulcis.

From those bright man - sions nev - er to roam; Oh, soon will time's dark
From the dear Sa - vior ne'er let us roam; Oh, soon will these dark

waves roll o'er us, Soon shall our loved ones greet us at home! Oh,
days roll o'er us, Soon shall our loved ones greet us at home! Oh,

soon shall time's dark waves roll o'er us, Soon shall our loved ones
soon will these dark days roll o'er us, Soon, &c.

greet us at home! At home, at home.........

......at home, at home.........

Allarg.

greet us at home, greet us at home...........

Poco        poco.        Morendo.

# COME HOME!

Wrighton.

Dolce.

p

f

3. Among my peo - ple you may dwell, Come home, come home! Rest in the church I love so well, Come

1. Hark, hear the Savior's gentle voice, It calls, come home! No longer make the world your choice, Come
2. Let childhood, youth, and hoary age, Come home, come home! Fear not the storms that round you rage, Come

p

home, come home! 'Twas for Her I once hung bleeding, Now in Heaven in - ter - ceding,

home, come home! Break the ties that long have bound thee, Leave the foes who would confound thee,
home, come home! Bid farewell to earth's vain fol - ly, Come to Me, the meek and low - ly,

For her welfare I am pleading, Come home, come home! Hark, &c.

Fly the dangers that surround thee, Come home, come home! Hark, hear the Sa - vior's
I will make you pure and ho - ly, Come home, come home! Hark, &c.

gen - tle voice, It calls, come home! No

long - er make the world your choice, Come home,.......... come home!

# COME UNTO ME.

Foley Hall.

1. Come un-to me, ye heav - y la-den! Come, young and old, for shel - ter to me!
2. Come un-to me, my prom - ise nev - er, Nev - er can fail, I've sealed it with blood;

Come, fie-ry youth, and gen - tle maiden, Come, freely come, and wel-come shalt thou be.
Those whom I love I love for - ev - er, Rest on my word, for I will make it good.

Life's darkest hours my love can bright - en, Soon will they come to the
Let not a doubt nor fear op - press thee, Nev - er can one of my

hearts now so gay ; The soul's heav-y load my help can lighten, Oh, fly to me, e'er
words pass a - way, O! let not the griefs of life dis - tress thee, Though dark thy night, I'll

comes the stormy day ! I am the friend to whom you must flee ; I am thy Sa - vior, oh,
turn it in - to day. I am, &c.

come un - to me. I am thy Savior, oh, come unto me !

# I HEARD A VOICE.

Scotch Melody.

**Allegretto.**

3. Now earth, of late so gloom-y, Bright glo-ry seems to wear, And

1. I heard a voice of warning, It whispered in my ear, And it
2. I sank beneath life's bur-den, And yielded to de-spair, And had

all things smile a-round me, Be-cause the Lord is near; Be-

bade me pause and pon-der, Be-cause the Lord was near; Be-
dark-ened all my spir-it, Be-fore I was a-ware; Be-

cause the Lord is near, I'll nev - er more de - spair, For He
cause the Lord was near, And loved to hear my prayer, And would
fore I was a - ware, But now re - lief was near, For the
f
on - ly came to save me, And on Him I'll cast my care.
ev - er guard and guide me, If on Him I cast my care.
gracious Help - er saved me, And on Him I cast my care.
Dim.
Cres.

# SORROW SHALL BE KNOWN NO MORE.

Stephen Glover.

**3.** But let me wait my Fa-ther's will, And take my share of good and ill, Wait

**1.** The glo-rious time is coming fast, When all life's dan-gers will be past, When
**2.** I would not choose my por-tion here, Mid earth's un-wholsome at-mos-phere: I

pa-tient-ly my hour of rest, My Fa-ther know-eth what is best. Then come what may, I'll

I from sin shall be set free, Oh! hap-py day! when shall it be? Soon shall I dwell in
long to breathe the air of Heaven, My pass-ions calmed, my sins for-given. That bless-ed home I

not re-pine, But lean up-on the arm di-vine; Soon life's hard bat-tle will be o'er, And

per-fect love, As ho-ly an-gels dwell a-bove; Soon life's hard bat-tle will be o'er, And
long to see, With ho-ly souls I long to be, When life's hard bat-tle shall be o'er, An

sor - row, sor - row will be known no more, sor - row will be known no more,
A tempo.
Dolce.
sor-row, sor-row will be known no more, sorrow will be known no more,
sor - row, sor - row shall be known no more, sor - row shall be known no more,
pp
A tempo.
p
Sor-row will be known no more, Soon life's hard bat - tle will be o'er, And sor-row will be known no
Cres.
Ritard.
a tempo.
Sorrow will be known no more, For soon life's bat - tle will be o'er And sor-row will be known no
Sor-row shall be know no more, When life's hard bat - tle shall be o'er, And sor-row shall be known no
Cres.
Ritard.
p
p
more.
more.
f
sf
f
sf
>

# "IT IS I!"

John Blockley.

3. It is I! and I will nev-er Send thee grief thou canst not

1. It is I! let no re-pin-ing In your mourn - - ful souls have
2. It is I! oh, then with glad-ness, Bear thy burd - - en brave-ly

*p*

bear; Thou art mine, and I will ev-er O'er thee watch with tend-'rest

birth; Know you not my kind de-sign-ing Is to wean you from the
on; Life's short hours waste not in sad-ness, Squan-der not so rich a

care. And at last, through my good Spir-it, Thou the king - - dom shalt in-

earth? Not one tear un-seen is fall-ing; None in vain on me are
boon. In my gar - - den I have placed thee, With my arms of love em-

*mf*

her - it,   Where the Fa - ther   dwells a - bove,   With the chil - dren of his   love.   **CHORUS.** It is

call - ing;   For I chas - ten   whom I   love,   Sor - rows but   my mer - cy   prove.   It is
braced thee,   There to   la - bor   and to   wait,   Pa - tient - ly   to bear thy   fate.   It is

*p*

I !   let no re - pin - ing,   In your mourn - ful souls have birth;   Know you not   my kind de -

I !   let no re - pin - ing,   In your mourn - ful souls have birth;   Know you not   my kind de -

*mf*

sign - ing,   Is to   wean   you from the earth?   It is   I !                It is   I !
**Rall. E Dim.**                **Ad Lib.**

sign - ing,   Is to   wean   you from the earth?   It is   I !                It is   I !

*mf*          *mf*

# WHERE'ER WE GO.

H. S. Thompson.

3. This is not our home, where we sad - ly roam, With fee - ble steps and

1. From the world on high, God's all - pierc - ing eye, Looks down on things be -

2. With a Fa - ther's love, from his throne a - bove, He sends us joy or

slow; Yet in this dark land, we've a friend at hand, Where - ev - er we may go.

low; And he sees us all, both great and small, Where - ev - er we may go.

woe; Let us all con - fide in this heav'n - ly guide, Where - ev - er we may go.

**CHORUS.**
Soprano.
Ad lib.

Where - ev-er— where - ev-er— where - e'er we go; He is

gaz - ing on us from his bless-ed a-bode, And he sees us where-e'er we go.

# I'LL NEVER DESPAIR.

H. S. Thompson.

4. Thy gift, the love as strong as death, Which ho - ly martyrs

1. Oh God, my heart is faint and weak, And wav'ring is my
2. And Thou canst give tho steadfast faith Of ho - ly men of
3. 'Tis Thine, when all is cold and dead, To bid the sin - ner

felt, As calm - ly, by the funeral pile, With upward glance they knelt.

faith ; But Thou canst give thy children strength To triumph o - ver death.
old, Who did, through un - told fu - ture years, The prom - i - ses be - hold.
live, And Faith, and Hope, and Char - i - ty, They all are Thine to give.

**CHORUS.**

I'll ne - ver de - spair though the tem - pests war, And the waves of sor - row

I'll ne - ver de - spair though the tem - pests war, And the waves of sor - row

rise; I'll look be - yond the storms of earth, To my home a - bove the skies.

rise; I'll look be - yond the storms of earth, To my home a - bove the skies.

# HAVE PITY ON THE POOR.

S. Glover.

1. How ma - ny poor and sor - row - ful, Are scattered far and near! As
2. This world is full of suf - fer - ing, Though beau - ti - ful it seems; And

Je - sus said, 'tis e - ver true, The poor are al - - ways here. Then clothe and feed all
there are woes for hu - man hearts, Be - yond our dark - est dreams. Turn not a - way, from

Rall.  A Tempo.

those who need, God will the gift re - store; 'Tis sweet to give; then while you live, Have
those who pray For mer - cy at your door; 'Tis sweet to give; then while you live, Have

pi - - - ty on the poor! 'Tis sweet to give; then while you live, Have
pi - - - ty on the poor! 'Tis sweet to give; then while you live, Have

pi - ty on the poor!
pi - ty on the poor!

3.

Remember Jesus, while on earth,
Was poor and lowly too;
Then let us all, for His dear sake,
The deeds of mercy do.
We cannot heal, we can but feel;
Heart-wounds we cannot cure;
But we can give; and, while we live,
Have pity on the poor.

# LOVE EACH OTHER.

English Melody.

Moderato con espress.

1. If the hearts of all men were but burning with love, How pleasant this world soon would grow!.... If we
2. Let us think of the great love of Je - sus, our Lord, Who gave up his glo - ri - ous home;.... Who was

all would a - gree like the Master to be, O then heaven would begin here be - low.......
lone - ly and poor, and the cross did en - dure, That we all to that glo - ry might come......

**Chorus.**

Then let us be lov - ing, for - giv - ing, and kind, As the Sa - vior of

Then let us be lov - ing, for - giv - ing, and kind, As the Sa - vior of

sin - ners has taught; . . . . And nev - er, nev - er more be to

sin - ners has taught; . . . . And nev - er, nev - er more be to an - ger in - clined, But be gen - tle in deed and in thought.

an - ger in - clined, But be gen - tle in deed and in thought.

**3.**

When the Lord was reviled, he reviled not again,
  But meekly his sorrows he bore;
And as pity and love brought him down from above,
  Let us pity and love evermore.
    Then let us, &c.

**4.**

For the meek ones of earth are beloved of the Lord,
  And blessed are they who forgive,
'Tis God's beautiful plan that the merciful man
  At the last his reward shall receive.
    Then let us, &c.

**5.**

Let the widow and fatherless never in vain
  For love and for sympathy sue;
Let us do unto all on whom trouble may fall
  As we wish that to us they should do.
    Then let us, &c.

# "POOR EXILES."

J. Blockley.

1. Poor ex - iles from our Fa - ther's home, We dwell in the stranger's
2. Then let us raise our tear - ful eyes A - bove all ter - res - trial

land; But comfortless we cannot roam When He leadeth us with his hand; Poor exiles from our
things, And for a flight to yonder skies, Let us plume our drooping wings; Then let us raise our

But comfortless we cannot roam When He leadeth us with his hand; Poor exiles from our
And for a flight to yonder skies, Let us plume our drooping wings; Then let us raise our

Father's home, We dwell in the stranger's land; But comfortless we cannot roam When he leadeth us with his
tearful eyes A - bove all ter - res - trial things, And for a flight to yonder skies, Let us plume our drooping

Father's home, We dwell in the stranger's land; But comfortless we cannot roam When he leadeth us with his
tearful eyes A - bove all ter - res - trial things, And for a flight to yonder skies, Let us plume our drooping

hand; For eve - ry day Over life's rugged, dangerous road; And we shall share
wings; The world of light Welcoming an - gels from above Are al - ways near,

hand; He smoothes the way, Over life's rugged, dangerous road; His
wings; is just in sight, Welcoming an - gels from above our

Till we rise to His blest a - bode............ Poor exiles from our Father's home, We
Far a - way to the home we love............... Then let us raise our tearful eyes A-

watch - ful care, Till we rise to His blest a - bode........... Poor exiles from our Father's home, We
souls to bear, Far a - way to the home we love............ Then let us raise our tearful eyes A-

dwell in the stranger's land; But comfortless we cannot roam, When He leadeth us with his hand.
bove all ter - restrial things; And for a flight to yon - der skies, Let us plume our drooping wings.

dwell in the stranger's land; But comfortless we cannot roam, When He leadeth us with his hand.
bove all ter - restrial things; And for a flight to yon - der skies, Let us plume our drooping wings.

# EVENING SONG.

S. M. Grannis.

3. So, with peace in the depths of the spir-it, To-geth-er we'er sing-ing our

1. Ho-ly Father! with praise and thanksgiving, While fadeth the light of this
2. May the an-gels of God be a-round us, A-far from us dan-ger to

song, For peace was the le-ga-cy left us By him un-to whom we be-long. Long

day, We come with a song to thy presence, And still for thy blessing we pray. Thy
keep, To ward off the pow-ers of darkness, And thus may we peace-ful-ly sleep, And

nights in the lone - ly, cold mountains, He watched, for the world of his love ;    But now, on the throne of his

fa-ther - ly care did preserve us, And gave us the sunshine so bright, Oh, by thy great mercy de -
rise in the bright ear-ly morn - ing, With spir-its all greate-ful to thee,    Who thro' the dark hours did

glo - ry,    He watch - es o'er all from a - bove, He watch-es o'er all from a - bove.
Ad lib.

fend us,    From per - ils and dan-gers this night, From per-ils and dangers this night.
keep us,    Who al - ways our Keep - er will be, Who al-ways our Keep - er will be.

# BLESSED ARE THE MEEK.

C. W. Glover.

1. To all the humble - heart-ed, A bless-ing Je-sus gave; On earth they have a
2. Oh ye, who strug-gle proud-ly, Un - wil - ling to be tried; The an-guish that you

Moderato.

por - tion, And one be - yond the grave. Their hearts are calm and peaceful, They en - vy not the
suf - fer, Is meant to break your pride. Your souls can - not be saved, Till pa - tient - ly you

great, They nev - er vain - ly murmur, But re - signed they meet their fate. They know th' - al - migh -
bow Un - to the will of Heaven; So 'tis well to suf - fer now, Lest, when your last hour

Fa - ther, Their hap - pi - ness doth seek, They know the Lord has prom - ised, His bless - ing to the
com - eth, In vain God's help you seek, But oh, the Lord has prom - ised, His bless - ing to the

meek, Has prom-ised, His bless-ing, his bless-ing to the meek, Has promised, His
meek, Has prom-ised, His bless-ing, his bless-ing to the meek, Has promised, His

blessing, his bless-ing to the meek.
blessing, his bless-ing to the meek.

# COME TO THE SAVIOR'S BREAST.

M. A. Browne.

3. Come, come, come! Come to that peace-ful home, Where God your souls will meet, With

1. Come, come, come! Come to the Savior's breast, Ye hea-vy la-den, come! He
2. Come, come, come! Come to the church of God, The pur-chase of his Son, For

true re-pent-ance come, Low-ly bow at Je-sus' feet. Join that great com-pa-ny Who, on

prom-is-es you rest, And a bright e-ter-nal home. The spir-it and the Bride To the'
in that dear a-bode You will nev-er feel a-lone. A cloud of wit-ness-es Will for-

earth, and who, in heaven, Praise the Lord e-ter-nal-ly, Their trans-gressions all for-given. Come, come, come!

wea-ry heart say come! And Christ the cru-ci-fied, Bids the wand'rer cease to roam. Come, come, come!
-ev-er greet you there; And the suff'ring heart feels ease When it breathes that sa-cred air. Come, come, come!

Join that great com-pa-ny Who, on earth, and who, in heaven,   Praise the Lord e - ter - nal -

Come  to the Savior's breast, Ye heav-y  la - den come !   He prom - is - es  you
A  cloud  of . wit - ness-es Will for - ev - er  greet you there ;   And the suffer-ing  heart feels

ly,   Their trans-gress - ions  all for - given.

rest,   And a  bright, e - ter-nal home.
ease   When it  breathes that sa - cred  air.

# THE ONLY SON.

B. Covert.

1. Gaz - ing back on years de - part - ed, Sat a moth - er, lone - ly heart - ed,
2. Cold the wea - ry heart was grow - ing, Bit - ter cold the wind was blow - ing,

Down her cheek sad tears had start - ed; Wept she for an on - ly son; Not one word her
Forth to Heav'n her prayer still go - ing, Wept she for an on - ly son; "Fa - ther!" cried she,

lips were say-ing, Reasons for her grief be-traying, But her earnest heart was pray-ing, For her lost, for-
watch thou o'er him, Smooth life's rugged path be-fore him, Soon to my fond arms re-store him, Save my lost, for-

sak-en one.
sak-en one.

### 3.

While she wept her hope grew brighter,
While she prayed her heart grew lighter,
Tempests could no longer fright her,
    Hoped she for her only son;
Soon her earnest prayer was granted,
God soon gave her what she wanted,
In her arms she clasped, enchanted
    Her long-lost, forsaken one.

### 4.

Ye who go through life despairing,
Never hoping, always fearing,
Hear this mother's voice so cheering,
    Telling of her only son;
God's kind care is never sleeping,
He is still his promise keeping,
Hope and pray, whenever weeping
    For some lost, forsaken one.

# "TROUBLED HEART."

M. S. Pike.

Dolce e Legato.

Soave.

Rall.

3. Sing for joy! Sing for joy! Tears must fall no more! For he who in the Lord con-

Troubled heart! troubled heart! Why so full of gloom? And why so sad - ly do you
'Twas for thee, 'twas for thee, The dear Redeem - er came; The sad - dest heart may sing for

Dim.

fides, Has countless joys in store. Why should the troubles of the earth Of a - ny moment seem, When

take Your journey to the tomb? O know you not a brighter home A-waits you at the end, Where
joy, Through his most ho - ly Name! He came to heal the broken heart, To dry the falling tear, To

soon    these transi - to - ry things          Will   vanish like  a    dream ?      Troubled  heart !

you     may dwell for-ev - er - more .          With your Almigh - ty   Friend ?    . Troubled  heart !
chase   a - way the gloom of   night,           And life's dark road to    cheer.      Troubled   heart !

Troubled heart !   Why   so  full  of   gloom ? And why   so   sadly  do  you  take     Your

*Dim.*

jour - ney  to   the   tomb ?

*Rall.*

# "THE CHURCH OF GOD."

J. W. Cherry.

Moderato con espressione.

3. The Church of God! Through Jesus' love In sweet com - mun - ion here may

1. The Church of God, I love her well! And to her bo - som would I
2. The Church of God! Oh, blessed home, Where I can al - ways sheltered

meet The saints be - low with those a - bove, All bowing at their Savior's

fly, Whene'er the waves of sorrow swell, And when the tem - pest frowneth
be! Why should I ev - er wish to roam A - way from joy, a - way from

feet, All bowing at the Savior's feet. My weary heart! now sat - is - fied, Here shalt thou
nigh, And when the tem - pest frowneth nigh! The Ark of God! up-on the wave She rides se-
thee? A-way from joy, a - way from thee? My Savior here in beauty dwells, Here dwell the
8va
rest, thy wand'rings o'er! Here peaceful - ly shalt thou a - bide, And fear the storms of earth no
cure and peaceful - ly, With room enough the world to save, With o - pen door all wide and
ho - ly and the good; And God his won - drous love reveals, Here in His Church redeemed with
Loco.
more, Here peaceful - ly shalt thou a - bide, And fear the storms of earth, of earth no more.
Espress.
Ad lib.
free, With room enough the world to save, With o - pen door all wide, all wide, and free.
blood, And God his won - drous love re - veals Here in His Church redeemed, redeemed with blood.
fz
Colla voce.

# WEARY AND FAINTING.

J. E. Carpenter.                                                    J. P. Knight.

1. Wea - ry and fainting, come un - to me! Bound fast in your fetters, Oh,
2. Wea - ry and faint-ing, com - fort is near! Your weep - ing is o'er, I will

come and be free! Why lon - ger de-spair - ing, lone and for-lorn From the
dry...... eve - ry tear; I've loved thee, poor sin - ner, loved.... thee so well That I

friend of thy spir - it a - way should'st thou turn? A fa - ther-ly eye watches
came down to earth in af - flic - tion to dwell. You sure - ly will trust in my

thee　from a - bove,　A　fa - ther - ly voice　calls in　ac - cents　of love,　I will
mer - - cy and love,　You sure - ly　will seek　for　a　por - tion　a - bove; I will

break　all your fet - - ters, and you　shall be　free,　Ye wea - ry and fainting ! oh,
break　all your fet - - ters, and you　shall be　free,　Ye wea - ry and faint-ing ! oh,

Rall.　　　　　　　　　　　　　u tempo.

come　un-to me,　ye wea - - ry and fainting, Oh come　un - to me,　Wea - ry and faint - ing,

Colla voice.

wea - ry and faint-ing,     wea - ry and faint-ing, Oh, come    un-to me,

wea - - ry and faint - ing,    wea - - ry and faint - ing,    wea - - ry and fainting, Oh, come unto me.

*mf*        *p*     Rall.